W9-CKL-423

Help the Environment

Caring for Nature

Charlotte Guillain

Heinemann Library
Chicago Illinois

Customer Service 888-454-2279

Visit our website at www.heinemannraintree.com

Picture research: Erica Martin, Hannah Taylor and Ginny Stroud-Lewis
Designed by Philippa Jenkins
Printed and bound in China by South China Printing Company.
12 11 10 09 08
10 9 8 7 6 5 4 3 2 1

Library of Congress Cataloging-in-Publication Data
Guillain, Charlotte.
  Caring for nature / Charlotte Guillain.
    p. cm. -- (Help the environment)
  Includes bibliographical references and index.
  ISBN-13: 978-1-4329-0889-8 (hc)
  ISBN-13: 978-1-4329-0895-9 (pb)
  1. Nature conservation--Juvenile literature. I. Title.
  QH75.G867 2008
  333.95'16--dc22

                          2007041174

Acknowledgments
The author and publisher would like to thank the following for permission to reproduce photographs: ©Alamy pp. **13** (Carlos Davila), **23 middle** (ilian), **4 bottom left** (Kevin Foy), **20** (B. Mete Uz), **19** (Brandon Cole Marine Photography), **17** (Jim West), **4 top right**, **23 top** (Westend 61); ©ardea.com pp. **12**, **23b** (George Reszeter), **10** (Paul Van Gaalen); ©Brand X Pixtures p. **4 bottom right** (Morey Milbradt); ©Corbis p. **11** (Simon Marcus); ©Digital Vision p. **4 top left**; ©naturepl.com p. **6** (Aflo); ©Photoeditinc. p. **5** (Michael Newman); ©Photolibrary pp. **15** (Animals Animals, Earth Scenes), **22** (Digital Vision), **21** (Image Source Limited), **14** (Juniors Bildarchiv), **16**, **18** (Mark Hamblin), **7** (Photodisc), **9** (Rodger Jackman), **8** (Stephen Shepherd).

Cover photograph of a butterfly on a flower reproduced with permission of ©Getty Images (Taxi, David McGlynn). Back cover photograph of a boy looking at a stag beetle reproduced with permission of ©Alamy (B. Mete Uz).

Every effort has been made to contact copyright holders of any material reproduced in this book.
Any omissions will be rectified in subsequent printings if notice is given to the publishers.

Contents

What Is the Environment?

The environment is the world
all around us.

We need to care for
the environment.

What Lives in the Environment?

Plants and animals live in
the environment.

Plants and animals are part
of nature.

Ways to Help the Environment

Bees need wild flowers.

When we do not pick wild flowers,
we help bees.
We help the environment.

Butterflies need wild flowers.

When we do not pick wild flowers,
we help butterflies.
We help the environment.

Birds lay eggs in nests.

When we do not touch nests,
we help birds.
We help the environment.

Birds need water to drink and wash.

When we put water in our garden,
we help birds.
We help the environment.

Litter can hurt animals.

When we pick up litter,
we help animals.
We help the environment.

Wild animals need to be left alone.

When we do not feed them,
we help wild animals.
We help the environment.

We can care for nature.

We can help the environment.

How Are They Helping?

How are these children caring for nature?

Answer on p. 24

Picture Glossary

 **environment** the world around us

 **litter** things we do not need any more

 **nature** plants, animals, and other things in the world that are not made by people

Index

Answer to question on p.22: The children are picking up litter. This will stop animals from being hurt by it.

Note to Parents and Teachers
Before reading
Talk to children about plants and animals in the environment. Have they seen wild flowers growing? Have they seen a wild animal like a squirrel or a fox?

After reading
• Make a waxed paper butterfly ornament. Draw the outline of a butterfly onto waxed paper. Shave some wax crayons and arrange the shavings in a symmetrical pattern on the butterfly wings. Cover the butterfly with another piece of waxed paper. Cover with a dish cloth and iron on using a low heat. Cut out the butterfly. Put a piece of string at the top and hang near a window.
• Make a bird feeder. Tie string to a large pinecone. Mix together some birdseed, oats, and peanut butter. Roll the pinecone in the mix and hang from a branch near a window where you can watch the birds feeding.